© **CELEBRATE LIFE WITH A SMILE**
BY SANDEEP RAVIDUTT SHARMA

Table of Contents

Foreword IV

Celebrate life with a Smile.....................................1

© **CELEBRATE LIFE WITH A SMILE**
BY SANDEEP RAVIDUTT SHARMA

Foreword

This book provides you with a list of **100** quotes and thoughts about LIFE, churned out by my mind with the consciousness, grace and energy of Shiva Shakti. I'm sure if you keep reading, referring, sharing these thoughts and quotes about LIFE, you may derive inspiration and develop good understanding of various perspectives and facts. Every moment, the wheel of life takes you forward to meet opportunities or threats. You need to learn how to respond with positive attitude and overcome life challenges, making the most out of life.

"Celebrate life with a Smile and make this world amazing."

I sincerely hope, you will find this book amazing, interesting, rejuvenating, unique and a constant source of Inspiration.

Thank You and Happy Reading.

© CELEBRATE LIFE WITH A SMILE
BY SANDEEP RAVIDUTT SHARMA

© **Copyright 2018 Sandeep Ravidutt Sharma - All rights reserved.**
In no way is it legal to reproduce, duplicate, or transmit any part of this document in either electronic means or in printed format. Recording of this publication is strictly prohibited and any storage of this document is not allowed unless with written permission from the publisher. All rights reserved. The information provided herein is stated to be truthful and consistent, in that any liability, in terms of inattention or otherwise, by any usage or abuse of any policies, processes, or directions contained within is the solitary and utter responsibility of the recipient reader. Under no circumstances will any legal responsibility or blame be held against the author / publisher for any reparation, damages, or monetary loss due to the information herein, either directly or indirectly. The author own all copyrights.

Legal Notice:
This book is copyright protected. This is only for personal use. You cannot amend, distribute, sell, use, quote or paraphrase any part or the content within this book without the consent of the author or copyright owner. Legal action will be pursued if this is breached.

Disclaimer Notice:
Please note the information contained within this book is for motivational, educational and knowledge sharing purpose only. Every attempt has been made to provide the reader accurate, up to date and reliable complete information. No warranties of any kind are expressed or implied. Readers acknowledge that the author is not engaging in the rendering of legal, financial, medical or professional advice. By reading this document, the reader agrees that under no circumstances the author / publisher is responsible for any losses, direct or indirect, which are incurred as a result of the use of information contained within this document, including, but not limited to, —errors, omissions, or inaccuracies.

If you have further questions, contact on **Tel: +919969256731**
Email: sandeepraviduttsharma@gmail.com

> © **CELEBRATE LIFE WITH A SMILE**
> BY SANDEEP RAVIDUTT SHARMA

Dedication

This book is dedicated to **Shiva Shakti** - the epitome of love. Lord Shiva is pure consciousness symbolising the masculine principle. Goddess Shakti symbolises the active feminine energy of Shiva and is synonymously identified with **Tripura Sundari, Sati** or **Parvati**.
These primal principles are also called as PURUSHA representing consciousness and PRAKRITI denoting the nature. Shiva and Shakti are manifestations of the all-in-one divine consciousness. Shiva is the paternal love of God that gives us consciousness, knowledge and clarity. Shakti is the motherly love of God that showers warmth, care and ensures our protection. Shiva and Shakti exist within each of us as the masculine and feminine energy. To please **Shiva Shakti** praying for the well being, love, happiness, strength, positive energy and success of my readers in their life, i hereby recite the following mantra...
"Sarva Mangala Mangalye Shive Sarvartha Sadhike Sharanye Tryambake Gauri Narayani Namostute"

© CELEBRATE LIFE WITH A SMILE
BY SANDEEP RAVIDUTT SHARMA

Photo Credits

The beautiful and amazing photograph used for the book cover is clicked by **Christina Tina Thorildsson** from **Sweden**.

You can visit her excellent photo gallery at **Instagram: @tinathorildsson**

CELEBRATE LIFE WITH A SMILE

© CELEBRATE LIFE WITH A SMILE
BY SANDEEP RAVIDUTT SHARMA

Your best is on its way.
Keep going with a Smile.

© CELEBRATE LIFE WITH A SMILE
BY SANDEEP RAVIDUTT SHARMA

Feel good and be ready to do better by giving your best.

© **CELEBRATE LIFE WITH A SMILE**
BY SANDEEP RAVIDUTT SHARMA

Celebrate the gift of life by living it to the fullest.

The element of surprise is lost when one knows the result before others. Keep surprises for the other.

© CELEBRATE LIFE WITH A SMILE
BY SANDEEP RAVIDUTT SHARMA

Celebrate each moment and be happy.

Those who love learning don't fear failures but sees it as an opportunity to learn further.

Becoming a rising star is fantastic achievement but maintaining the shine is commendable.

Dictate terms only when consent doesn't work.

Absorb the goodness to create and share more.

© **CELEBRATE LIFE WITH A SMILE**
BY SANDEEP RAVIDUTT SHARMA

Your flaws make you human. Accept them with a vow to improve.

Build the castle in the air if you like vanishing act and not when you decide to live in.

Tears roll out when you feel the presence of the Lord in whatever you do and whichever way you decide to go.

Love brings joy in your life.

Look at challenges as opportunities to grab and grow.

© CELEBRATE LIFE WITH A SMILE
BY SANDEEP RAVIDUTT SHARMA

Beautiful mind creates awesome thoughts.

Dance to the tune of life with enthusiasm and you won't repent.

Celebrate solutions by resolving the problems.

Resolve conflict with ease. All you have to do is change your self instead of trying to change the other.

Sea of opportunities waits for none. You need to act in time and earn them.

Things would work out well when you have self-belief and trust in the Lord.

Those who are deeply in love never bind the other.

One who seeks challenges is not afraid of it.

Appeal to the Lord for justice instead of expecting it from man.

What caused pain today may bring joy on some other day.

Reveal your plan if it can mobilise forces to achieve the aim.

© **CELEBRATE LIFE WITH A SMILE**
BY SANDEEP RAVIDUTT SHARMA

You feel blessed when you keep chanting Lord's name.

© CELEBRATE LIFE WITH A SMILE
BY SANDEEP RAVIDUTT SHARMA

Exploring life fascinates the curious mind.

Expressing regret when you are wrong keeps the relationship intact.

Your words can make a friend out of a stranger.

© CELEBRATE LIFE WITH A SMILE
BY SANDEEP RAVIDUTT SHARMA

Drive darkness with light of knowledge.

You don't have to run after success but lead.

Everyone is ready to share your achievements and happiness. Hardly few would dare to share grief and sorrow.

Luck never runs out for those who keep going with hope.

Efforts are not an option unless you plan to buy Success.

Many of us are hesitant even to express our likeness, forget about love for the other.

The joy of living comes only when you live in the present.

Celebrate freedom of choice by choosing wisely.

Do good things and regrets are no more.

First you should trust those from whom you expect trust back.

The ocean of thoughts is good when it creates pearls of wisdom.

What started as a hobby can become your profession if you pay attention.

Worry is no more when you worship the Lord with Love and devotion.

Wishes from the heart are invaluable for the receiver.

Your wishes make someone's day and bounces back to you golden gratitude.

Fight for your rights following the righteous path.

© CELEBRATE LIFE WITH A SMILE
BY SANDEEP RAVIDUTT SHARMA

Feed the hungry if you can.

World ends for you only when you decide to give up. Keep trying and you can Win.

Act smart if you can deliver what you have promised.

The future holds the mystery while your actions create it today.

As you walk with amazement, beautiful things are coming your way.

Always follow what is right, and not what seems to be right.

Planting a seed takes few minutes while nurturing is a life long process.

© CELEBRATE LIFE WITH A SMILE
BY SANDEEP RAVIDUTT SHARMA

Celebrate life by sharing happiness and without any return expectations.

Narrate your story if it's interesting and someone is listening.

Always practice hard before you appears for the test. Over confidence hardly helps. Hard work always pay.

Celebrate your achievements by announcing to the world.

Relationship based on trust and love last forever.

Number of words spoken hardly matters, it's the message that counts.

Don't do everything for your own success, do things sometimes which makes the other win.

Give your best to pass the test.

Find your life purpose, achieve it and celebrate.

Understand the process to produce the desired result.

Just try to Smile when pain looks at you.

Not everyone has the capacity to learn from criticism and take a vow to improve. Those who do are the winners.

Celebrate the moment you are breathing in.

Ride on the horse of knowledge to reach destination of Wisdom.

The bond of love strengthens with caring attitude.

Celebrate life as it comes to you.

© CELEBRATE LIFE WITH A SMILE
BY SANDEEP RAVIDUTT SHARMA

If you read and remember the story, it was worth the read to share.

Wonderful are the ways of the Lord. One plants seed for the other to enjoy the shade.

Wonderful are the ways of the Lord. You embark on your journey, and he decides about your destination.

Those who love you from the bottom of their heart can never make you cry.

Make an impact with your actions instead of trying to impress the world.

© CELEBRATE LIFE WITH A SMILE
BY SANDEEP RAVIDUTT SHARMA

Celebrate the colours of life by staying positive with vibrant thoughts.

Everything happens at its own time and with a purpose. Don't rush in to do it instantly.

Self-motivation is an ongoing process.

Achieve success on your own ability and not by pulling others down.

Accept your shortcomings with a vow to replace them with strength in time.

Your choice in life decides whether you flourish or perish.

© CELEBRATE LIFE WITH A SMILE
BY SANDEEP RAVIDUTT SHARMA

The talented person may not be Smart, but a Smart person can use someone's talent.

Those who build in silence are not dumb but intelligent ones who believe that their work will speak.

© **CELEBRATE LIFE WITH A SMILE**
BY SANDEEP RAVIDUTT SHARMA

Join the caravan of happiness by staying joyful and absorbing goodness.

Celebrate goodness by spreading kindness.

Change your situation by harnessing the constructive power of the mind.

Don't let someone's criticism carry your intelligence to the remote island. Thank your critics and use your intelligence to do course correction if required.

© CELEBRATE LIFE WITH A SMILE
BY SANDEEP RAVIDUTT SHARMA

Celebrate your differences by agreeing to disagree.

Do things which challenges you and celebrate when they are no more.

Mind rusts when it is deprived of beautiful thoughts. Feed good thoughts and keep it fresh always.

Match the curiosity of a child, and nothing would be impossible.

Celebrate grace and glory by respecting women.

Million thanks to the Lord for giving us this day.

Don't hide your expressions if you want the right response.

True friends never need an invite whether one celebrates or mourns.

Things are changing every minute. Those who can anticipate or create change are likely to benefit.

Curiosity makes you learn.

Live now with peace in your mind, love in your heart, humility in your words and hands full of efforts.

Greater confidence takes time to build. Take one step at a time.

© CELEBRATE LIFE WITH A SMILE
BY SANDEEP RAVIDUTT SHARMA

Payback in gratitude when your money is not worth enough to compensate for someone's selfless contribution.

Live one day at a time with full honesty and commitment. This habit can forge the long-term relationship.

Celebration never stops for those who are living in the present.

www.ingramcontent.com/pod-product-compliance
Lightning Source LLC
Chambersburg PA
CBHW031439210526
45464CB00005B/2267